WORKBOOK

Summary, Lessons & Action Prompts

FOR

The Happiness Advantage: How a Positive Brain Fuels Success in Work and Life

A Practical Guide to Implementing Shawn Achor's Book with Action Prompts

Marc Glover

Copyright © 2023 **Marc Glover**

Disclaimer

Please note that this publication is an independent creation by Marc Glover and is not authored by Shawn Achor, nor is it affiliated with them. Carefully crafted, this enlightening overview and interactive workbook provide meticulous insights and profound analysis of the original book.

Our aim is to equip readers with invaluable insights and ignite a journey of exploration into the core concepts of the primary work. It is essential to understand that this publication is not a replacement for the original piece. We strongly recommend readers to obtain the original work for a comprehensive understanding of the subject matter.

Table of Contents

How To Use This Book? 2

Overview Of The Book 5

Chapter 1: Discovering the Happiness Advantage 9

    Chapter Summary: 9

        Key Lessons: 9

        Action Prompts (Reflective Questions): 11

        Life-Changing Exercises: 16

Chapter 2: The Happiness Advantage at Work 17

    Chapter Summary: 17

        Key Lessons: 17

        Action Prompts (Reflective Questions): 19

        Life-Changing Exercises: 24

Chapter 3: Principle #1 - The Happiness Advantage 26

    Chapter Summary: 26

        Key Lessons: 26

        Action Prompts (Reflective Questions): 28

        Life-Changing Exercises: 33

Chapter 4: Principle #2 - The Fulcrum and the Lever 35

    Chapter Summary: 35

        Key Lessons: 35

        Action Prompts (Reflective Questions): 37

Life-Changing Exercises: 42

Chapter 5: Principle #3 - The Tetris Effect, Identification of Possibility Patterns...44

    Chapter Summary: 44

    Key Lessons:...45

    Action Prompts (Reflective Questions):...46

    Life-Changing Exercises: 50

Chapter 6: Principle #4 - Falling Up...52

    Chapter Summary: 52

    Key Lessons:...52

    Action Prompts (Reflective Questions):...54

    Life-Changing Exercises: 59

Chapter 7: Principle #5 - The Zorro Circle 61

    Chapter Summary: 61

    Key Lessons:...61

    Action Prompts (Reflective Questions):...63

    Life-Changing Exercises: 67

Chapter 8: Principle #6 - The 20-Second Rule...69

    Chapter Summary: 69

    Key Lessons:...69

    Action Prompts (Reflective Questions):...71

    Life-Changing Exercises: 76

Chapter 9: Principle #7 - Social Investment...78

Chapter Summary: 78

   Key Lessons: 78

   Action Prompts (Reflective Questions): 80

   Life-Changing Exercises: 85

Chapter 10: The Ripple Effect 87

   Chapter Summary: 87

      Key Lessons: 87

      Action Prompts (Reflective Questions): 88

      Life-Changing Exercises: 93

Free Gift

Unleash the power within you with a complimentary copy of our captivating book, designed to spark your potential and propel you toward excellence.

Scan the QR Code below to secure your free copy today:

DOWNLOAD NOW!

Discover the ultimate solution to break free from automatic negative thoughts!

Ready to get started?

Scan the QR Code below!

How To Use This Book?

Here is the workbook that goes along with Shawn Achor's book "The Happiness Advantage: How a Positive Brain Fuels Success in Work and Life". With the aid of this workbook, you will be able to go further into the concepts presented in the book, actively engage with the material, and apply these life-changing concepts to your situation. Here are some tips for getting the most out of this workbook:

- Chapter Summary: Before diving into the workbook exercises, review the material covered in each chapter summary, which offers a succinct synopsis of the main ideas covered in "The Happiness Advantage."

- Key Lessons: Consider the most important takeaways from every chapter. Think about the connections between these realizations and your goals and experiences.

- Action Prompts (Reflective Questions): The purpose of the reflective questions is to promote self-reflection and introspection. Spend some time thinking carefully about these prompts and examining your feelings, ideas, and personal experiences that are connected to the subjects covered.

- Life-Changing Exercises: Complete the hands-on activities that are included in each chapter. These exercises are practical steps based on the ideas presented in the book. Incorporate them into your everyday routine to develop a positive outlook, improve your overall health, and create a more satisfying existence.

- Use this workbook as a personal journal for introspection. When you complete the activities, keep a journal of your ideas, realizations, and development. Go back over your reflections from time to time to see how you've changed and to recognize your successes.

- Share and Connect: Think about letting people know about your discoveries and advancements. Talking about your adventure with loved ones, coworkers, or friends might improve your education and bring you new insights.

- Remain Consistent: Change requires patience and perseverance. Decide to go through this workbook methodically. Make time for the content regularly to ensure a gradual but significant change in your perspective.

Recall that your active engagement in this workbook is the key to getting the most out of it. Accept the exercises with an open mind and a desire to consider alternative viewpoints. You are investing in your development as you work through these pages, but you are also opening the door to a more fulfilled and prosperous existence. Start the journey now!

Overview Of The Book

Finding true pleasure and success can seem like an impossible goal in the fast-paced world we live in when stress and negativity seem to be on the rise. In this difficult environment, Shawn Achor's ground-breaking book, "The Happiness Advantage: How a Positive Brain Fuels Success in Work and Life," provides a ray of light. Achor's empirically supported observations and useful tactics highlight a basic fact: happiness is not only a desired byproduct of success but also a potent inducer of it. We are urged to reconsider our opinions as readers and to welcome the capacity for positive thinking to change.

Book Summary:

"The Happiness Advantage" transports us to the field of positive psychology, where Achor dispels popular belief about happiness and success with a fascinating array of data. Achor contends that happiness drives success, defying the widespread assumption that happiness follows success. Based on a wealth of research, including studies carried out in many global settings, he shows how developing a positive brain can improve general well-being, creativity, and productivity.

Achor's teachings are even more relevant during global difficulties, such as financial crises and personal disappointments. He delves into the notion of the "Happiness Advantage," which postulates that having an optimistic outlook improves our capacity for growth, adaptation, and inventiveness. Through an exploration of seven fundamental concepts, such as the Zorro Circle, the Tetris Effect, and Social Investment, Achor offers useful methods for rewiring our minds to become more optimistic.

The Use of this Workbook:

As we absorb the knowledge presented in "The Happiness Advantage," the question of how to use these life-changing concepts naturally comes to mind. This workbook is the result of that investigation. It originates from a strong sense of duty to disseminate the profound influence of Achor's lessons in a useful, doable manner.

This workbook is a customized manual meant to support individual development rather than just a supplement to the primary material. It is designed to assist readers in internalizing the main ideas, considering their personal experiences, and applying the ideas in practical contexts. Readers will go on a transforming journey through thoughtfully chosen exercises, questions, and activities, peeling back the layers of their attitude and realizing their enormous potential.

As we traverse the obstacles of contemporary society, this workbook turns into an invaluable resource for anybody pursuing contentment, perseverance, and achievement. Readers may apply the happiness advantage to their own lives and promote good change at work, home, and in their communities by actively participating in the material.

You'll find a plethora of exercises and tools motivated by Achor's remarkable insights in the pages that follow. Accept this workbook as your unique road map to a more contented and prosperous existence. Let's set off on a life-changing journey together to rewire our brains for happiness and unleash the endless opportunities that lie ahead.

Chapter 1: Discovering the Happiness Advantage

Chapter Summary:

Shawn Achor challenges the belief that happiness follows achievement in "Discovering the Happiness Advantage," providing strong evidence that happiness comes before success. Rewiring our brains for optimism and happiness is crucial, as Achor underlines with a combination of scientific findings and real-world applications. This chapter lays the groundwork for the life-changing adventure that lies ahead, teaching readers how minor adjustments to habits and thinking can result in big improvements in a variety of spheres.

Key Lessons:

- Happiness is the Fuel for Success: Happiness is the fuel for success, not the key to happiness. Performance and achievement can be fueled by an optimistic attitude and a positive mindset.

- The Tetris Effect: We can rewire our brains to recognize patterns of opportunity, which will enable us to recognize and take advantage of opportunities everywhere we look.

- Social Investment: Having a robust social support system can enhance one's success and well-being.

- Ripple Effect: Improving general happiness and productivity can be achieved by implementing positive change within our families, businesses, and teams.

- Small Changes, Big Gains: Making minor adjustments to one's behaviors and way of thinking can have a big impact on one's career, personal life, and health.

Action Prompts (Reflective Questions):

After reading this chapter, in what ways has your understanding of the correlation between success and happiness changed?

_____

_____

_____

_____

_____

_____

_____

_____

_____

_____

Would you desire to alter any pessimistic tendencies in your life? How can you identify areas for improvement using the Tetris Effect?

_____

_____

_____

_____

_____

_____

_____

_____

_____

_____

Think about your circle of social support. Are there any steps you can take to make it stronger? How can you put more of a social stake in the welfare of others?

_____

_____

_____

_____

_____

_____

_____

_____

_____

_____

Consider the beneficial alterations you hope to see in your family, neighborhood, or place of employment. What actions can you take to start a positive chain reaction?

_____

_____

_____

_____

_____

_____

_____

_____

_____

_____

What minor adjustments to your daily schedule or perspective can you do to leverage the happiness advantage in your life?

_____

_____

_____

_____

_____

_____

_____

_____

_____

_____

_____

Life-Changing Exercises:

- To increase your positive vibes, start a gratitude diary and write down three things you are grateful for every day for the next 21 days.

- Use the Tetris Effect by resolving to identify and take advantage of one opportunity or happy moment every day for a month. Follow your development.

- Make contact with a friend or coworker you haven't spoken to in a while, and cultivate that friendship. Become more socially invested.

- Launch a positive challenge in your family or place of employment. Urge people to share their good news, special occasions, or everyday deeds of kindness.

- To make a little but meaningful difference in your well-being, pick one habit or practice. Make a plan to put that change into action, and then monitor your advancement over time.

Chapter 2: The Happiness Advantage at Work

Chapter Summary:

In the book "The Happiness Advantage at Work," Shawn Achor explores the use of positive psychology concepts at work. He investigates how happiness cultivation might boost output, inventiveness, and general success in the workplace and life. Achor provides strong evidence that an optimistic outlook is crucial for both personal and professional success, as well as being a vital component of well-being.

Key Lessons:

- Positive Work Environment: Fostering a positive work environment increases employee engagement, which raises output and contentment.
- Optimism Promotes Innovation: People with an optimistic outlook are more inclined to solve

problems imaginatively and inventively, which promotes a continual improvement culture.

- Resilience in Adversity: Building resilience enables people and groups to overcome obstacles with a positive outlook and to recover from setbacks.

- Collaboration and Social Support: Establishing strong social ties at work fosters teamwork, collaboration, and overall job performance while also fostering a positive work atmosphere.

- Happiness as a Competitive Advantage: Organizations that place a high priority on employee happiness and well-being can attract and retain top talent, which boosts overall success.

Action Prompts (Reflective Questions):

How can you help your team or company create a more happy work environment?

_____

_____

_____

_____

_____

_____

_____

_____

_____

_____

How does your present state of mind affect how you handle opportunities and problems at work?

_____

_____

_____

_____

_____

_____

_____

_____

_____

Think back to a difficult scenario you have at work. In what ways could adopting a more positive outlook assist you in solving problems or managing comparable circumstances in the future?

_____

_____

_____

_____

_____

_____

_____

_____

_____

_____

_____

Think of your network of professional contacts. Exist opportunities to improve relationships with coworkers on a social level? How can these partnerships be fostered?

_____

_____

_____

_____

_____

_____

_____

_____

_____

_____

What programs or modifications to the workplace could you propose to put the pleasure and well-being of your employees first?

_____

_____

_____

_____

_____

_____

_____

_____

_____

_____

_____

Life-Changing Exercises:

- Keep a Gratitude Journal: Every day, write down three aspects of your job or coworkers that you are grateful for. Regularly consider these favorable characteristics.

- Positive Affirmations: To help you maintain a positive outlook, make a list of affirmations that are relevant to your professional objectives and repeat them every day.

- Random Acts of Kindness: Show your coworkers that you appreciate them by showing real gratitude or by offering assistance when needed. Take note of the effect on your well-being and the environment at work.

- Strengths Assessment: Determine your strongest suit and figure out how to apply it to your activities at work. Making use of your strengths increases self-assurance and professional fulfillment.

- Mindful Breaks: During work breaks, engage in brief mindfulness exercises or breathing exercises to improve focus and lower stress levels, which will contribute to a more positive work environment.

Chapter 3: Principle #1 – The Happiness Advantage

Chapter Summary:

In this section of "The Happiness Advantage," Shawn Achor delves into Principle #1: The Happiness Advantage. He explores the enormous effect that happiness has on our capacity for success in a variety of spheres of life. Achor questions the conventional wisdom that happiness follows achievement and provides strong evidence that happiness precedes success. People can significantly improve their productivity, creativity, and general well-being by rewiring their brains to be more positive, which will give them an advantage in both work and life.

Key Lessons:

- Happiness Drives Success: Developing an optimistic outlook increases motivation, fosters success, and builds resilience in the face of adversity.

- Positive Brain Chemistry: Practicing happiness increases focus, creativity, and problem-solving skills by releasing neurotransmitters like serotonin and dopamine.

- Optimism Drives Achievement: People with optimism are more likely to aim high, stick with a plan in the face of failure, and eventually accomplish amazing feats.

- Impact on Society and the Workplace: Contented people often cultivate wholesome connections, establish encouraging work environments, and serve as role models for others, which spreads happiness and prosperity.

- Mindset Matters: Having a positive outlook not only improves one's well-being but also modifies perceptions, opening doors and producing positive results.

Action Prompts (Reflective Questions):

For you, what does happiness mean? Think about how your definition of happiness affects your objectives and desires.

_____

_____

_____

_____

_____

_____

_____

_____

_____

_____

Determine Positive Influences: Think about the people, things, or circumstances that make you happy. How can you use more of these components in your day-to-day activities?

_____

_____

_____

_____

_____

_____

_____

_____

_____

_____

_____

Challenging Negative Thoughts: Recognize any limiting ideas or negative self-talk. How might you reinterpret these ideas to promote a happier perspective?

_____

_____

_____

_____

_____

_____

_____

_____

_____

_____

Make a gratitude list of three things for which you are thankful every day. How does this practice affect your outlook and general state of mind?

_____

_____

_____

_____

_____

_____

_____

_____

_____

_____

_____

_____

Establishing Positive Intentions: Make a positive intention for the day by concentrating on your goals and desired frame of mind. How is your experience shaped by this intention?

_____

_____

_____

_____

_____

_____

_____

_____

_____

Life-Changing Exercises:

- Daily Positive Diary: Keep a daily diary in which you can jot down accomplishments, happy memories, and expressions of thankfulness. Regularly go over these entries to reaffirm happy feelings.

- Random Acts of Kindness: Do little deeds of kindness for people, such as offering a compliment, a helping hand, or a consoling word. Keep an eye on how these behaviors affect both your mood and the responses of the recipients.

- Visualization Technique: Take some time each day to picture your dreams and ambitions as though they have already come true. To increase the efficacy of this technique, involve your emotions and senses.

- Set aside time for mindfulness meditation, when you concentrate on the here and now without passing judgment. Observe how this exercise improves your general feeling of happiness and well-being.

- Gratitude Visit: Make contact with someone who has improved your life and offer your appreciation. Express your gratitude in writing, via email, or in person, and see the positive emotional ripple effects of this relationship.

Chapter 4: Principle #2 – The Fulcrum and the Lever

Chapter Summary:

In Principle #2 of "The Happiness Advantage," Shawn Achor examines the ideas of the lever and the fulcrum as symbols for our attitudes toward obstacles. Knowing that our thinking serves as a pivot allows us to use it to our advantage to overcome challenges and succeed. Achor highlights the influence of perspective on results, showing how a positive outlook functions as a lever to increase our capacity to overcome obstacles and improve our general well-being.

Key Lessons:

- Mindset as Fulcrum: Our thoughts act as the pivot or fulcrum that drives our behaviors and responses. Positive thinking is a conscious choice, and it has the power to shape our experiences.

35

- Leveraging Positivity: Positivity serves as a lever that increases our resilience and capacity for problem-solving. It enables us to take on obstacles with grit and inventiveness.
- Reality Is Shaped by Perception: Our reactions are strongly influenced by how we view a certain circumstance. Developing an optimistic outlook can turn obstacles into chances for development.
- Flexibility & Adaptability: When faced with difficulty, a positive outlook makes us more flexible and enables us to change course and modify our approach.
- Self-Efficacy: Self-belief in our capacity to overcome obstacles fortifies our determination. Thinking positively increases self-efficacy, which gives us the courage to take on challenging activities.

Action Prompts (Reflective Questions):

Evaluation of Mindset: Consider the main perspective you have when faced with difficult circumstances. Is it typically neutral, negative, or positive? How does this way of thinking affect your feelings and behaviors?

_____

_____

_____

_____

_____

_____

_____

_____

_____

_____

Positive Reframing: Contemplate a recent obstacle that you overcame. How can you change the way you see the situation—from bad to good? What chances for development and education show up?

_____

_____

_____

_____

_____

_____

_____

_____

_____

Analyze your current obstacles in life by conducting an obstacle analysis. How may an optimistic outlook serve as a tool to overcome this obstacle? List possible options that are motivated by optimism.

_____

_____

_____

_____

_____

_____

_____

_____

_____

_____

_____

Exercise for Visualization: Envision yourself confidently and easily conquering a major challenge. What actions can you take to make this image a reality after being inspired by it?

_____

_____

_____

_____

_____

_____

_____

_____

_____

Journaling about your thinking: Write down any instances over the week when you felt that your mindset had an impact on your experiences. Observe how having an optimistic outlook affected your regular encounters and capacity for problem-solving.

_____

_____

_____

_____

_____

_____

_____

_____

_____

_____

Life-Changing Exercises:

- Gratitude Exercise: Keep a gratitude notebook and write down three things for which you are thankful every day. This practice increases optimism and directs attention toward the good things in life.

- Positive Affirmations: Make a list of affirmations that are specific to the areas in which you want to develop. Reiterate these statements daily to strengthen your positive belief system.

- Struggle Reframing: Write a brief tale about a recent struggle you overcame victoriously. This practice develops resilience and stimulates original problem-solving.

- Mindfulness Meditation: To improve your mental control and self-awareness, engage in mindfulness meditation. Consistent meditation fosters a serene and optimistic frame of mind.

- Random Acts of Kindness: Make it a habit to perform random acts of kindness. Small acts of kindness toward others bring happiness to everyone around you and not only help to encourage positivity.

Chapter 5: Principle #3 - The Tetris Effect, Identification of Possibility Patterns

Chapter Summary:

The Tetris Effect is a phenomenon that occurs as our brains get skilled at identifying patterns and chances in daily life is covered in "The Happiness Advantage,". This chapter explores how our minds may be trained to recognize recurring patterns to detect possibilities and capture opportunities. The chapter draws inspiration from the popular computer game Tetris. People can improve their general optimism, inventiveness, and problem-solving skills by developing this talent.

Key Lessons:

- Learning to spot patterns in different settings might help you find possibilities that may otherwise go unnoticed.

- Positive Focus: The Tetris Effect highlights the value of cultivating an upbeat attitude in life by concentrating on positive patterns.

- Enhanced Creativity: Seeing opportunities stimulates creativity, which helps people come up with original solutions to problems.

- Adaptability: Mastering the Tetris Effect improves adaptability, making it easier for people to deal with change and uncertainty.

- Mindset Shift: Changing one's perspective from one that is negative to one that is positive enables people to see possibilities when others may only see barriers.

Action Prompts (Reflective Questions):

What recurring themes have you seen in your day-to-day activities that can present chances for development or enhancement?

_____

_____

_____

_____

_____

_____

_____

_____

_____

In your personal and professional efforts, how can you use the Tetris Effect to change your perspective from obstacles to opportunities?

_____

_____

_____

_____

_____

_____

_____

_____

_____

_____

_____

Think back to a recent instance where you were able to solve a problem by identifying a pattern. What insights did that experience give you?

_____

_____

_____

_____

_____

_____

_____

_____

_____

_____

Exist any unfavorable thought or behavior patterns that prevent you from moving forward? How can you substitute constructive patterns for them?

_____

_____

_____

_____

_____

_____

_____

_____

_____

_____

_____

Think about a target you are aiming toward. How can you find smaller steps or patterns that lead to its achievement by using the Tetris Effect?

_____

_____

_____

_____

_____

_____

_____

_____

_____

_____

_____

Life-Changing Exercises:

- Pattern notebook: For a week, keep a notebook in which you record any recurrent themes or patterns in your ideas, conversations, and actions. Determine which positive patterns to emphasize.

- Positive Pattern Visualization: Set aside ten minutes every day to visualize success and identify successful patterns in your thoughts. Observe the effect on your viewpoint in general.

- Make an opportunity mind map by examining possible prospects in both your personal and professional spheres. Determine the links between various opportunities and the best ways to explore them.

- Struggle Transformation: Write down any possible benefits or lessons you learned from a recent struggle you overcame. Practice applying the Tetris Effect to transform obstacles into opportunities.

- Gratitude Pattern: Consider times in your life when you were thankful regularly. To reinforce good thinking, make a gratitude collage or diary to visually depict these patterns.

Chapter 6: Principle #4 - Falling Up

Chapter Summary:

In "Falling Up," Shawn Achor delves into the notions of resilience and growth that follow traumatic experiences. He explores how people can overcome obstacles and setbacks to not only return to their pre-problem status but also reach a higher degree of fulfillment and functioning. Adversity and failure should be welcomed as chances for growth and learning, according to Achor. He provides examples of how developing resilience can result in significant improvements in our lives.

Key Lessons:

- Resilience as Strength: Developing resilience gives us the tools to deal with life's obstacles and disappointments, promoting mental and emotional fortitude.

- Accepting Failure: Reinterpreting setbacks as opportunities for growth and development allows us to evolve, adapt, and learn from our experiences.
- Post-Traumatic Growth: Adversity can act as a stimulant for human development, resulting in a more meaningful existence, richer relationships, and heightened self-awareness.
- Mindset Matters: Cultivating optimism, reinterpreting setbacks, and concentrating on solutions rather than issues are all part of building a resilient mindset.
- The Function of Support: Overcoming hardship and developing resilience is greatly aided by social support and deep relationships with others.

Action Prompts (Reflective Questions):

Taking on Difficulties: Consider a previous difficulty you overcame. What abilities or talents did you gain from the experience, and how did it affect the way you see upcoming difficulties?

_____

_____

_____

_____

_____

_____

_____

_____

_____

_____

Failure as a Teacher: Contemplate a recent mishap or disappointment. What takeaways are there from this event, and how can you use these takeaways in other contexts?

_____

_____

_____

_____

_____

_____

_____

_____

_____

_____

_____

Post-Traumatic Growth: Think back to a trying time in your history. How has this event changed your priorities, enhanced your sensitivity, or helped you grow personally?

_____

_____

_____

_____

_____

_____

_____

_____

_____

_____

Recognize the problem you are currently experiencing with a resilient mindset. How can you reframe this challenge so that it becomes a chance for personal development and education?

_____

_____

_____

_____

_____

_____

_____

_____

_____

_____

_____

Creating Cordial Relationships: Assess your network of support. Who are the people in your life that you can rely on when things get hard? How can you make these connections stronger?

_____

_____

_____

_____

_____

_____

_____

_____

_____

_____

Life-Changing Exercises:

- Resilience Journal: Keep a journal in which you record difficult circumstances you encounter, your feelings during them, and the lessons you take away from them. Consider how you have evolved throughout time.

- Take on the Fear-Conquering Challenge: Decide which discomfort or fear you have been putting off. Make a tiny step toward facing it, accepting the discomfort, and thinking back on the encounter afterward.

- Gratitude Exercise: Establish a routine of thankfulness. Even on the bad days, list three things for which you are grateful each day. This exercise cultivates optimism and resilience.

- Capabilities Assessment: Determine your unique set of abilities and capabilities. Participate in activities that take advantage of these assets regularly to increase your resilience and self-assurance.

- Expand Your Support Network by Reaching Out to Someone You Look Up To and Thanking Them for Their Work or Accomplishments. Developing relationships with influential people can be a great way to get support and inspiration.

Chapter 7: Principle #5 – The Zorro Circle

Chapter Summary:

In this enlightening chapter, Shawn Achor explores the idea of narrowing our attention and making baby, doable actions in the direction of transformation. He takes his cues from Zorro's tale, reminding us that we can reclaim our sense of control and widen our sphere of influence by first focusing on manageable, tiny areas. This idea highlights how important it is to begin small, get the hang of things, and then progressively increase our efforts to accomplish bigger objectives. It's an effective method for gaining momentum and confidence in both our personal and professional lives.

Key Lessons:

- Start Small, Dream Big: We set ourselves up for major success by focusing our efforts on doable activities that are under our control.

- Confidence by Competence: When we are proficient at modest things, we feel more confident and can take on more difficult ones.

- Focus Increases Effectiveness: By focusing on a small area of impact, we can more efficiently use our energy and produce better outcomes.

- Gradual Expansion: After we have the hang of things, we may confidently take on bigger challenges by progressively widening our sphere of influence.

- Mindful Progress: Keeping an eye on our accomplishments, no matter how tiny, inspires us and helps us stay motivated.

Action Prompts (Reflective Questions):

Which particular aspect of your life or career would you like to enhance?

_____

_____

_____

_____

_____

_____

_____

_____

_____

_____

What modest, doable actions can you do in this domain to increase your expertise and self-assurance?

_____

_____

_____

_____

_____

_____

_____

_____

_____

How do you narrow your concentration so that you can become proficient at these smaller tasks?

_____

_____

_____

_____

_____

_____

_____

_____

_____

_____

_____

What hindrances or diversions could impede your advancement and what steps can you take to alleviate them?

_____

_____

_____

_____

_____

_____

_____

_____

_____

How are you going to monitor your advancement and acknowledge even the most minor successes along the way?

_____

_____

_____

_____

_____

_____

_____

_____

_____

_____

Life-Changing Exercises:

- Zorro Circle Visualization: Shut your eyes and see a circle that symbolizes your present point of focus.

Within this circle, pick one modest, doable objective and picture yourself achieving it.

- Daily Zorro Tasks: Decide on one Zorro Circle-related duty to complete each day. Prioritize finishing this assignment before tackling any other obligations.

- Progress Journal: Record your everyday accomplishments inside your Zorro Circle in your journal. Consider how these little victories advance your main objectives.

- Provide a detailed plan for growing your sphere of influence in the circle. Determine the abilities or information you must obtain to effectively take on more difficult tasks.

- Accountability Partner: Tell a mentor or close friend who can hold you accountable about your Zorro Circle objectives. Frequent check-ins will offer inspiration and support.

Chapter 8: Principle #6 – The 20-Second Rule

Chapter Summary:

Shawn Achor explores the idea of removing obstacles to good transformation in his investigation of the 20-Second Rule. He highlights the importance of making it harder to participate in bad habits while increasing the time and effort required to establish beneficial ones. People can modify their behavior and mentality significantly and achieve long-term success and happiness by realizing the power of lowering activation energy.

Key Lessons:

- Activation Energy Is Important: The amount of work needed to begin an activity has a big influence on whether or not it is completed. Positive behaviors are easier to establish and more accessible when their activation energy is lower.

- Behavior is Shaped by Environment: Depending on how you change your surroundings, some actions may be encouraged or discouraged. Setting up a setting that supports healthy behaviors encourages consistency and long-lasting transformation.
- Consistency Outweighs Intensity: Over time, little, consistent acts produce significant change. Positive habits that are simple to establish will be easier to stick with over time.
- Conscientious Space Design: By carefully planning your environment, you can encourage productive and upbeat behaviors while impeding negative ones.
- Tiny modifications, Big Impact: You may significantly increase your level of productivity and pleasure by making even small modifications to your routine or surroundings.

Action Prompts (Reflective Questions):

What bad habits do you wish to get rid of, and how can you make it take more energy to indulge in them?

_____

_____

_____

_____

_____

_____

_____

_____

_____

_____

_____

Choose one virtuous behavior you would like to develop. How can 20 seconds be easier to start and keep going over time?

_____

_____

_____

_____

_____

_____

_____

_____

_____

_____

Think about the places you work and live. Do they support constructive behavior? If not, what adjustments can you do to promote virtuous behaviors and discourage bad ones?

_____

_____

_____

_____

_____

_____

_____

_____

_____

_____

Think of your everyday schedule. Where can you effectively introduce new, positive behaviors by using the 20-Second Rule?

_____

_____

_____

_____

_____

_____

_____

_____

_____

_____

Consider your social network. How can you surround yourself with people who help you stick to your good habits by encouraging and supporting you?

_____

_____

_____

_____

_____

_____

_____

_____

_____

_____

_____

Life-Changing Exercises:

- Conduct an environment audit to assess the conditions at home and at work. Determine the things that get in the way of good behaviors. Make these adjustments right away to get rid of the barriers.

- Habit stacking is the process of incorporating a new, virtuous habit into an already-existing routine. To make it very simple to start, apply the 20-Second Rule.

- Visible Cues: Make your surroundings a visible reminder of your objectives and virtuous routines. To motivate positive behavior and reaffirm your intentions, use items, photos, or sticky notes.

- Digital detox: Lower the activation energy required to turn off digital gadgets at particular times of the day. Establish dedicated areas free from screens to promote unwinding and sincere interactions.

- Choose an accountability partner who shares your objectives, such as a friend or relative. Regularly update each other on your progress and hold each other responsible. It might increase dedication and motivation to know that your efforts are being noticed by someone else.

Chapter 9: Principle #7 – Social Investment

Chapter Summary:

The idea of social investment is a cornerstone of success and pleasure in the field of positive psychology. Shawn Achor highlights in this chapter the significant influence that fostering meaningful relationships has on our general well-being. In addition to being a source of happiness, social ties are crucial drivers of both professional and personal development. Achor explores how strong social links may improve resilience, increase happiness, and spur success in both work and life as she digs into the science of healthy relationships.

Key Lessons:

- The Power of Meaningful Connections: Strong, meaningful bonds foster emotional resilience by serving as a protective barrier against stress and misfortune.

- Quality Wins Out Over Quantity: Creating a small number of solid, sincere connections has a greater influence than growing a vast network of phony connections.
- Support and Reciprocity: Putting money into other people's well-being encourages a mutually beneficial atmosphere that builds a network of people who can lean on in trying times.
- Shared Positivity Multiplies: Developing positive relationships increases happiness for everybody involved since pleasant feelings are contagious.
- Relationship Emotional Intelligence: Bonds are strengthened and harmonious interactions are produced when one can recognize and relate to the emotions of others.

Action Prompts (Reflective Questions):

Consider Your Social Circle: Assess the quality of the connections you currently have. Which ones provide you the most happiness and encouragement? How come?

_____

_____

_____

_____

_____

_____

_____

_____

_____

Acts of Kindness: What good deeds can you do for your friends, family, or coworkers? Think about little actions that convey your gratitude and regard for them.

_____

_____

_____

_____

_____

_____

_____

_____

_____

_____

_____

Resolution of Conflicts: Do your relationships still have unsolved conflicts? Consider how to resolve these disputes in a way that promotes stronger relationships.

_____

_____

_____

_____

_____

_____

_____

_____

_____

_____

Practice Empathy: Imagine yourself in the position of a close friend or relative. What would they think of your words and deeds? Consider your conversations from their point of view.

_____

_____

_____

_____

_____

_____

_____

_____

_____

_____

_____

Creating New Connections: Determine the spheres of your life in which you can encounter people who share your values. Which pastimes, pursuits or social circles fit your values and interests?

_____

_____

_____

_____

_____

_____

_____

_____

_____

_____

Life-Changing Exercises:

- Write sincere letters of gratitude to those who have made a good difference in your life. Express your gratitude and appreciate their impact on your development and well-being.

- Quality Time Commitment: Make a regular time commitment to spend uninterrupted, concentrated time with your loved ones. Give real talks and family time a higher priority than online diversions.

- Random Deeds of Kindness: Every day, carry out acts of kindness at random. These might be anything from offering a neighbor assistance to praising a coworker. Keep an eye on how these behaviors affect your relationships and overall mood.

- Practice Active Listening: Make an effort to listen intently throughout conversations. Take a moment to ponder, and then thoughtfully reply to others. Observe how this method strengthens your relationships.

- Social Detox: Assess how your interactions on social media impact your overall health. Think about going cold turkey on social media for a while. Pay attention to face-to-face conversations and note how they affect your general level of happiness.

Chapter 10: The Ripple Effect

Chapter Summary:

Shawn Achor delves into the idea of the ripple effect in this chapter of "The Happiness Advantage," highlighting how happiness can change people on a universal level. Achor explores the ways that good feelings and deeds can spread, impacting not just our local environment but also the larger community. We improve our well-being and foster a pleasant, flourishing atmosphere when we share happiness.

Key Lessons:

- The Power of Positive Influence: Feeling good about ourselves and the people around us makes us feel good too, so we spread that feeling to others.
- Creating Social Connections: Deep connections strengthen the positive feedback loop, promoting a feeling of belonging and enjoyment among everybody.

- Motivating Positive Change: Mild deeds of generosity and optimism have the power to uplift others and set off a domino effect of positive actions.

- Building a Supportive Network: Being in the company of upbeat people amplifies the good ripple effect and starts a happy spiral that keeps going.

- Accountability for Collective Well-Being: Acknowledging our part in other people's happiness highlights the significance of purposeful optimism in all relationships.

Action Prompts (Reflective Questions):

In what ways—positive or negative—have you seen the ripple effect in your own life?

_____

_____

_____

_____

_____

_____

_____

_____

_____

_____

_____

_____

What deliberate steps can you take to make your family, place of employment, or community happier?

_____

_____

_____

_____

_____

_____

_____

_____

_____

_____

_____

_____

Think back to a time when you were greatly impacted by the beneficial influence of someone else's well-being. How can you do that for other people?

_____

_____

_____

_____

_____

_____

_____

_____

_____

_____

_____

_____

Think about your social network. Do you have any relationships that make a positive difference in your life? How can you strengthen these bonds even more?

_____

_____

_____

_____

_____

_____

_____

_____

_____

_____

_____

_____

How can you make your everyday routine more positive and kind-hearted acts of kindness to increase the ripple effect?

_____

_____

_____

_____

_____

_____

_____

_____

_____

_____

Life-Changing Exercises:

- Gratitude journaling: Keep a gratitude notebook where you may jot down everyday acts of kindness and happiness and consider how they affect your perspective and those around you.

- The Random Acts of Kindness Challenge is to do one random act of kindness every day and track the effects on the beneficiaries as well as yourself.

- Participate in volunteer work or community projects to actively improve the lives of others and see the positive ripple effect for yourself.

- Positive Communication: To create a more upbeat environment, use positive communication strategies in your interactions with others, such as active listening and encouraging language.

- Establish a Happiness Network: Choose people in your life who make you feel good and make a conscious effort to spend more time with them. Developing these connections will make the ripple effect in your social circle more pronounced.

Made in the USA
Middletown, DE
04 September 2024